A Dream... Once Upon A Quiet Mind

by Mahi

Sunstar
PUBLISHING LTD.

A Dream…
Once Upon a Quiet Mind
by Mahi

Sunstar Publishing, Ltd.
204 S. 20th Street
Fairfield, Iowa 52556

First Edition 1998

Printed in the United States of America

Library of Congress Catalog Card Number: 98-060182

ISBN: 1-887472-50-9

Cover & Text Design: Irene Archer

Readers interested in obtaining further information on the subject matter of this book are invited to correspond with:

The Secretary, Sunstar Publishing, Ltd.
P.O. Box 2211, Fairfield, Iowa 52556
More Sunstar books at: http://www.newagepage.com

Dedication

This book is dedicated to all those who live in quiet desperation. May you gain peace of mind…and the courage to dream again.

Acknowledgements

I would like to acknowledge Patricia Florin, Denise Poole, Irene Archer, Rodney Charles, my friends and all my family for their enormous contributions to this book. I am so grateful for all of you. Thank you for being here!

Who am I to experience joy?
Who am I to know fulfillment?
None other than the eternal dreamer.

Introduction

All of us dream...sometimes by day, sometimes by night. Life is the fulfillment of pleasant dreams for some, while for others, life stands out in stark contrast to what is hoped for. Too often, our joyful dreams are washed away by a nightmare of actual life.

We continue to allow our dreams to slip away as foolish thoughts, rather than embracing those thoughts and choosing to make them our waking reality. We even attempt to dream less, thinking that our innermost desire is the product of an over-active imagination. We misjudge our true feeling as that which distracts us from getting in touch with reality.

Growing up has come to mean denying intuition...forgetting rather than fulfilling dreams. Our mind has become separated from our heart, believing that 'waking life' and 'dreams' are separate. There is a growing gap, an unfilled emptiness, as we attempt to survive a reality which is so isolated from what we truly seek.

Disconnected from the heart of our being, we lack inspiration. Survival in the 'real' world becomes more difficult without the spirit of personal desire to motivate us. There comes a point where we lack the energy to sustain ourself...if what we've come to accept as 'reality' is all that there is to life.

Our heart was our energy source. Our dream was the purpose. Our desire was the spirit which energized the whole endeavor. As a child we knew that...but somehow, we have forgotten. No longer swimming in the ocean of deeper reality, we find ourselves drowning on the surface. We have managed to convince ourselves that surviving is the purpose. By accepting this illusion as our reality, we have too often abandoned our grandest dream and accepted a lesser dream. We have closed ourselves off from the very source of life...that which allows us to survive at all.

How long will we deny the passion burning within us, only to experience an outward hell? What if the outer struggle is the result of our perpetual outward focus. What if the outer world could be transformed by uniting our mind and hearts through the spirit of our dreams. What if that spirit would allow us to encounter life as whole beings, rather than disillusioned fragments.

The entire world has become fragmented. The alone mind sees a world of limits. Each person and each nation attempts to survive, rather than fulfill. Each one competes for what appears to be limited, rather than embrace what is unseen and therefore limitless.

As we listen to our heart, we are becoming aware that the fear and struggle of the outer world is a direct reflection of our internal struggles. When humanity feels torn within, we isolate ourselves from one another. As our dreams become isolated from daily life, our heart becomes isolated from our mind, and our desire becomes isolated from its fulfillment.

In February 1997, I experienced a dream. It was a combination of sleeping visions and waking thoughts. I seek to share this dream, not as another voice screaming from without, but as a reminder of Love whispering from within. I do not want to offer something to think about so much as to remind others to feel, and thereby know their own true wisdom.

This dream reminded me of my purpose...my desire...my passion. And thus I seek to inspire others to remember their own dreams. Those dreams are there now, moving within us, like tiny motion pictures, waiting to expand onto the big screen of life. By listening to our heart, we can feel the beat...tune into the rhythm...and be filled with the music of our own song. That heart is calling us.

Once upon a time I had a dream. It was after a day of work and worry, and I looked forward to rest. Upon falling asleep I found myself in a nightmare. I dreamed of a river that gushed through my home and abruptly washed me out of bed. I struggled frantically within the raging waters; it was cold and dark and I could not see where I was headed. Then I looked at the water itself. It was made of the very struggles and problems that I was experiencing in my life.

There, in the river, were the people who had hurt me, creditors wanting their money, and lovers asking me to change. There were the jobs that I hated yet worked at day after day, and the headaches, illnesses, and other ailments that bothered me. I was caught up in the river of a troubled life flowing out of control.

I looked up and saw that the river was flowing into the chest of an enormous monster. I was terrified when I realized that I would soon be swallowed up by this dark and fearsome looking creature. As the river carried me closer, the monster's face became clearer and seemed vaguely familiar. Recognition washed over me. I was shocked to see my own fearful face peering back at me.

As the river flowed into the monster's chest,

the motion stopped and the water vanished. Everything became still except for the beating of my heart. I sat motionless in the darkness. The surface below me was soft and warm. It felt like my own flesh.

In front of me I could hear a loud drumming sound which pulsed to the rhythm of my pounding heart. I realized that it was the sound of a heart beating in time to my own. I began to feel warm and peaceful in this environment. The sound of the heartbeat became softer and slower as I relaxed. It seemed as if another lifetime passed as I sat still and quiet.

Then out of the darkness a tiny light appeared. The light grew brighter until it revealed its source as a candle. Sitting behind the candle and looking into the flame was a being. The being looked like a person, but unlike any I had ever seen. This being glowed with life and youthfulness, yet at the same time appeared ancient and wise. In the background I could make out the faint outline of a large pulsating heart, still in rhythm with my own. Without looking up, remaining focused on the flame, the being spoke:

"You've been looking for me."

"I have? Who are you?"

"I am your heart and the source of your desire. I am also that which you desire most."

"What has happened to me? Am I dead?"

"Can you hear your own heart? Or are you still deaf to its voice?"

"Am I asleep then?"

"You have been asleep, even when you think you are awake. But at this moment, while you sleep, you are more awake than ever."

The being remained transfixed upon the flame. I could see the fire dancing in its eyes, becoming one with the light that appeared to emanate from them.

"So I'm having a dream," I concluded.

"Always."

"Can I ever awaken?"

"If you were to awaken in such a way as to dream no more, you would not exist. But you do exist."

"If I'm always dreaming, then what does it mean to be awake?"

"There are two kinds of dreams—the ones you think are real and the ones you know are a dream. It is when you think the dreams are real that you are most asleep. When you remember they are a dream, you are most awake. Those moments, when you know that your life is a dream and that you are the dreamer, are the closest you come to being awake."

"How can I believe you?"

"How can you believe anyone?"

"I don't know. How do we *come to believe anything?"*

"A good question. We come to believe something is true only through trust. You can believe me because I am your Self. I am your heart and the source of your deepest desire. But you need not trust me nor believe what I say. You have a choice. I do not force my will or my desire upon you."

"If you are my own heart and I don't trust you,

then who would I trust? If I don't believe you, then who would I believe?"

"You can believe someone else. You can believe what others tell you, but this is a choice. They cannot force you to believe them any more than I can force you to believe me."

"What do you mean you can't force me to believe you? What choice do I have if you are my Self? This is confusing."

"Confusion results when you ignore your heart. If you are confused, listen to your heart, and do not doubt the feelings of your heart with the thoughts of your mind. If you trust, you will know.

"By trusting, you will know the truth in your heart. If you doubt, you will look for knowledge in your mind. Trust does not require knowledge; trust is a feeling. Trust is wisdom from the heart."

"You're not helping much."

"That is because you still doubt me. You fear what would happen if you trusted your heart completely."

"But how is that possible? If I am talking to my Self, then how can I doubt you? Why don't I already know that you are me?"

"You do know, at least your heart does. In your heart you know who you really are. Your heart knows that you are a very powerful being, so powerful that if you doubt or choose to be afraid, you can experience that fear as real."

"Are you saying that I am afraid?"

"Yes, you are."

"What am I afraid of?"

"You are afraid of me. You are also afraid of the power you have to fulfill your desires."

"How do I know you're right?"

"Trust me. The truth is there really is no separation between us. You are one with me and I am one with you. Together we are one powerful being and we have the ability to create experience.

"Fear is just one of many possible experiences. The only way to have the experience of fear is to imagine it. Fear is a thought of the mind. The possibility of fear arises when you are so asleep that you think your current dream is all there is.

"When you fear, you create fear in your experience. A little fear may result in a bad dream. A great deal of fear can turn that dream into a nightmare. Your dreams are a reflection of you. Experiences have no reality or meaning except that which the mind chooses to give them. You are the writer, the painter, the sculptor, the dreamer of the dream.

"In a fearful dream, you think of your Self as limited to your mind. Through fear, the mind 'thinks' that it is separate from me, your heart. Fear causes your mind to feel as though it is limited and finite. This creates even more fear, the feeling that you are being hurt by the world and the experience of being vulnerable to its forces. The more your mind fears, the more it loses touch with its connection to me.

"In your heart you know that you are wise, indestructible, and eternal. I am the part of you that knows nothing can ultimately destroy you. However, through fear you can experience harm and all of the confusion, hurt, and suffering that fear causes in the mind.

"Fear creates a space between us, between the

mind and the heart. Spirit bridges the space between your mind and heart. During this dream, the heart and the mind continue to communicate through spirit.

"Sometimes the mind fears so greatly and forgets so completely that it denies both spirit and heart. But the heart never denies or forgets. The heart remembers the truth—that the mind, heart, and spirit are one. This is the true nature of the Self."

"So you're saying I wouldn't be having this conversation if I wasn't afraid. That you are my heart and source of desire and only appear to be separate from me because I am afraid."

"Yes. You are afraid, and your fear produces more fear and doubt. If you had no fear, you would not be questioning your heart, however, we would still communicate. If you lived in total trust, you would know oneness with me. You would know the desires of your heart without question.

"Through trust, your mind knows the 'thoughts' of your heart, which actually exist in the form of feelings. Feelings are the first thought—the intuition, the impulse, the spontaneous notion sent from the heart to the mind. Your first thought is the pure wisdom of unconditional Love. This Love is sent from the all-knowing universe where your heart lives.

"When this thought of Love is ignored, the mind goes to work to create knowledge. The mind literally builds walls of knowledge that isolate itself from the heart's wisdom. There is nothing 'wrong' with knowledge. But the mind that looks outside itself can only accumulate information, none of which is the true source of experience."

"Why do you allow this?"

"My desire is that the mind be free to choose and manifest its own will. This allows the mind to have the experience of 'becoming' .

"I contain the potential that allows you to become. The mind creates the sense of time as a result of creating events. The mind 'becomes' as it creates experiences and feels itself moving through time. The creative process is then complete."

"Has fear caused my soul to divide?"

"Yes, in a way. But this separation is an illusion. Fear causes the mind to feel disconnected from the heart. This feeling of isolation interrupts the creative process and the mind no longer has the experience of 'becoming'. Instead, the mind feels out of control and frozen by fear.

"Your 'soul' is another word for your true Self: your mind, heart, and spirit all in one. Your soul is not separate from your mind or body; however, fear causes your soul to feel divided."

"Where does my body fit in here?"

"Your body is an extension of your soul. The thoughts of your mind surface within your body instantly. If your soul were an ocean, your body would be the surface.

"When thoughts bubble up and rise to the surface of the ocean, they enter all parts of your body at once. Thoughts cause the energy or chemicals in your toes to change as well as the chemicals in your brain. Your entire body reflects the thoughts of your mind."

"I still don't understand how all of this works together to make me who I am."

"There are countless ways to describe who you are; you are limited only by the restraints that you imagine in your mind. Limits are a construct of your imagination. Through Love, your mind is able to transcend these limitations."

"How is that possible?"

"Your soul is a universe, a spherical universe with a heart at the center. As my energy of unconditioned Love radiates outward from the source, I am in the form of spirit. The mind takes some of this spirit energy and molds it to form a body. Each thought of the soul's mind forms a body of compact energy that circles around a center point or heart.

"The human body can be considered one thought that revolves around the heart of the earth. The earth itself is a thought revolving around the heart of the sun. The entire solar (soul) system is a thought that revolves around the heart of a galaxy. All of the galaxies are thoughts revolving around the heart of the Universal Soul.

"All of these revolving bodies of compact energy are thoughts formed out of spirit. The heart continues to radiate the spirit of unconditional Love energy. This energy sustains the various bodily forms within the Universal Soul.

"Energy flows from heart center to heart center. My Love flows from the heart of the universe to the heart of the galaxy. From there I flow to the sun or heart of each solar (soul) system. Then I flow to each planet and to the nucleus or heart of every atom which forms every fragment of matter on the planet. I radiate out from the core of every life form on earth. I am in the heart of every atom that forms the human body."

"Am I speaking to the heart of my human body or to the heart of the Universe?"

"Both, my friend. The language of Love is channeled from one heart to another. Understanding this is the beginning of wisdom.

"If the message is one of unconditional Love, then you know it is coming from the heart and an aspect of your own, true Self. If the message is one of fear, then you can be certain that the information is being made up by the mind.

"Love speaks of oneness and unifies all creation. Fear speaks of division and creates separation. The powerful message of Love flows from every heart. The limiting message of fear always comes from the mind."

"Why would anyone choose to communicate fear?"

"A person can only communicate that which he is experiencing. When the mind forgets the heart, a person loses his innocence—his inner sense of security and power. Thus, he attempts to gain control outwardly. Transcending this outer dilemma comes through a return to the heart and the awareness of the true nature of the soul.

"For the sake of simplicity and explaining your earthly experience, allow me to redefine the three aspects of the soul. There is the heart: the source of unconditioned Love and desire, which is fulfilled through experience. There is the mind, which includes your body: the realm of the soul in which experience occurs. And there is the spirit: the *feeling* which bridges communication between your heart and mind. Your heart, mind and spirit are one, and together they form your soul."

"Are you saying my soul also includes my body? Won't I release my body and keep my soul when I die?"

"When you die you will not cease to have a body; the body is just the surface of the ocean that is your soul. In truth, that which I refer to as your 'soul' is your 'real' body. Death is just a change in the mind of the soul."

"You say that you are the source of my desires. If that's so, what's the difference between the will of my mind and the desires of my heart?"

"When you 'will' to follow me there is no difference. When the desire of your heart and the will of your mind are one, you 'will' have the experience of being fulfilled. When you doubt your desire or doubt your heart, you doubt your Self. You are a powerful being. In order to experience fear or doubt you must separate from me."

"Am I powerful enough to separate from you totally?"

"Your mind can imagine that it is alone in the world and create an experience of separation that will seem absolutely real in your mind. But this experience is an illusion. You can't separate from me, because we are one. If you could truly separate from me, you would cease to exist. This is impossible."

"You said that already."

"Yes, and you continue to doubt."

"If I stop doubting, won't I cease to exist as a

mind that fears and doubts?"

"Precisely! You can't cease to exist entirely, but you can cease having fearful experiences. You are an experience, and the mind is a place to imagine such an experience. That which you know of as your body is the actualization of the experience.

"The human body is a place where the mind, heart and spirit have joined together to form a 'part' within the soul. This 'part' is created in the image of the whole. By being in the form of a body, the soul is able to experience other parts (bodies) and thus experience its Self. Experience is only possible through the existence of bodies in various dimensions of physicality.

"Physicality is a term used to describe the density of energy: how compact its particles are spiraling and vibrating together. By creating parts within the whole, or physical bodies of relative density, the soul can experience what it already knows in the heart.

"Now, my friend, can you begin to understand the unity of all beings within one soul? Everything is formed from the tri-unity of mind, heart, and spirit. This trinity is duplicated over and over again as each thought of mind becomes another heart center which sponsors another thought or experience of mind.

"For example, the sun is not only a thought of universal mind but also the heart of a solar (soul) system. The earth is not only a thought of the solar mind but also the heart of many other life forms and experiences. The human body is not just an earthly life form (thought) but also the heart of human experience. The human experience is not just a thought in the brain but exists as energy that emanates from the heart of every atom in the body."

"What happens when we die? Does the human being realize that it is you?"

"Your body dies in response to what your mind is thinking. In your mind you believe time is limited. You believe that your body is limited, so you create a body that is finite. This causes your body to experience death, changing the surface of your soul.

"It is in your body that your thoughts about reality surface to create an experience. So you die precisely because you do not remember me—your heart. The death of your physical body is not necessary for you to know me. Only the death of fear is required to know me, for it is only your fear that separates us.

"There are two kinds of death: one is the death caused by fear, resulting in constant rebirth into a world of fear. The second is the death of fear itself, resulting in the experience of being born into a world of Love."

"Is this the meaning of life?"

"I do not determine the meaning of life. It is up to you, the mind, to determine life's 'meaning.' However, you may consider spending less time worrying about life's meaning and more time enjoying the experience.

"Searching for meaning is an experience in and of itself, but it is not all of life. Life can be lived any way you choose to live it. By letting go of fear you can cease to question and analyze. This will allow your life to become a wonderful dream come true if you so desire."

"What is the best way to live my life?"

"Any way you choose. I have no preference."

"But I thought you were the source of my

desire? If you don't know, who does?"

"I am the source of your desire! And ultimately, there is only one desire—to experience the Self. All desires come from me and return to me, the heart of unconditional Love.

"When you choose to be consciously aware of me in your experience, then you only need to choose Love. Trust that you are the source of your experiences and nothing can harm you."

"That seems like a tall order!"

"For many it is a tall order. It is a struggle to let go of fear, and sometimes this struggle creates more fear. Then the mind often chooses to withdraw even further from the heart, to hide behind walls of doubt.

"The simple idea of choosing Love, trusting, and letting go of fear may speak against everything you have conditioned yourself to believe. But no one can rescue you from this dilemma. Each human being is the source of his own experience and must choose to listen to the heart to change that experience.

"This can be confusing at first. In order to hear one's own heart, all the layers of conflicting information that the mind has gathered must be sorted out. This knowledge may exist in the form of intellectual reasoning and arguments that the mind has used as weaponry to defend itself against the pain it believes to be originating from 'outside' itself.

"This rationalization may make perfect sense to the mind, as there are forces the body encounters in the world that actively attempt to harm others. What the mind has not yet realized is the ability to dismantle and recreate these forces into new experiences that are chosen by the person's own mind."

"How do I gain that realization?"

"The power to consciously guide and transform experience is gained by loving all things unconditionally. This power arises from the heart into the open mind."

"What must I know in order to Love in that way?"

"Nothing. You already know. The core of every being is Love. When feelings are honored and allowed to flow, a feeling of Love will emerge. This experience is diminished when the mind accepts thoughts that the heart is evil or that desires are wrong.

"What humans consider knowledge is often just a construct of fear. This knowledge may be in the form of memories that have been locked away in the mind, because of the pain they invoke for the individual. The mind may believe these memories are protecting it from harm. However, by holding on to fearful memories, the pain of the past is being re-created and experienced again in the present.

"This survival response results when the mind views each new situation through the filter of a fearful past experience. A person may think they are acting wisely by closing down their heart. In truth, the mind is over-reacting and perpetuating pain.

"Healing can only occur when the mind views the world through the eyes of unconditional Love. This involves becoming the creator of each new experience. It is only then that the soul can see things as they really are, experiencing the 'is-ness' of pure Love."

"Should I forget all knowledge?"

"It is not necessary to forget, but to understand. Awareness will allow you to use knowledge as a tool to create new experiences of joy, rather than experiences of survival.

"For example, having knowledge about the natural cycles of earth allows humans to live harmoniously and in balance with these cycles, embracing the opportunity for unique experience that this planet provides.

"Having knowledge about the beauty of the human form and the joy of human desire allows a person to embrace this glorious opportunity to be in a human body. Seen through the eyes of fear, knowledge can become a problem. Seen through the eyes of the heart, knowledge creates opportunity.

"Knowledge includes all thoughts of the universal mind that have created bodies of energy such as stars, planets and humans—with their fearful or loving beliefs. Wisdom is the awareness that these bodies of knowledge are created from the same energy.

"Wisdom reveals that there is nothing intrinsically good or bad about any part of the universe. Knowledge is a construct of the mind that creates an opportunity for experience. Knowledge combined with wisdom creates the joy of abundant experience and eternal life. This means functioning as a whole being by uniting the mind (knowledge) with the heart (wisdom) through the spirit."

"How do I gain wisdom?"

"By listening to your heart. At first, this can seem like swimming upstream. The mind is actually remembering the effortless flow of the heart.

"The mind that reconnects with the heart may go through a series of transformations as it removes the walls that it has worked so hard to create. While going through these changes it may feel as if the heart is asking the mind to experience the very pain it has tried to avoid. In reality, this pain was created by the mind that chose fear and doubt in the first place.

"During this process of returning to the heart, the mind will need to trust more than ever. It will need to focus on the heart to hear its voice. This voice may seem faint at first, like a whisper, barely audible. It may be indistinguishable from all the 'other' voices of the mind that scream out to be heard. Yet, when the mind remains focused on the heart, its voice can grow louder and stronger to rise above the other voices.

"When the heart's voice is heard clearly, the mind can then recognize the heart in every experience. Love will become the predominant voice, drawing more and more Love toward itself. Then the mind will need no more convincing because the power of Love will be understood through personal experience."

"Must we work through all the pain of the past to experience Love in the present?"

"Working through the pain of the past is not the way! Fear leads to doubt and causes the mind to work to protect itself from what it believes are 'things' that can hurt it. But it is by 'working' that the walls are erected between the heart and mind. Work did not begin until you began to doubt.

"The heart cannot be found when the mind works. The heart is discovered when the mind stops working and allows the heart to perform its miracles. The magic of the heart is realized by allowing it to be, not by the mind trying to control it.

"It is the difference between using a shovel to dig into the fluid core of the earth or allowing the red hot lava of Love to flow outward, melting away the rocks, ice, and sludge as it flows. One process requires struggle, the other is effortless.

"When the mind feels the heart's Love but still chooses to fear, pain is felt. The mind is afraid of losing a memory and losing itself. But Love only dissolves the pain of a memory. The heart can't erase a memory. It only washes away the sludge that fear has built up so that we can see and feel the experience clearly ... through the eyes of Love. The heart does not erase the Self, but rather, allows us to see the Self clearly, without fear or judgment.

"Fear wastes time and delays the healing process. Love knows no time like the present. For those who are willing to let go completely, healing can occur spontaneously, without effort or pain. Some choose such healing, and those who witness this choice call it a miracle."

"This means all the struggle and searching in my life has only taken me further away from you!"

"It is true that you do not need to 'search' for me, nor is there 'struggle' in my world. You only need trust to open the door to the heart. When the mind doubts, it searches and struggles, and doesn't get anywhere. Realizing this, it can choose to give up the struggle and just be. This is when the mind remembers its true source is the heart."

"Am I 'wrong' to deny you?"

"If you call fear wrong. But I do not judge any choice as right or wrong. Nor will I punish you someday for your choices, as there is no 'someday.' There is only this moment and the experience your choices provide you.

"The mind and the heart have a cause-and-effect relationship. The mind desires, believes and creates a certain reality and the heart gives the mind the experience of that reality."

"How can the mind be the cause, if you are the source of desire?"

"I am the source of desire, for without the heart, the mind would not have the potential to become. I am 'all desires fulfilled, all dreams realized.' But the heart does not make choices for the mind. The mind must choose which experience it wishes to have.

"The mind is always in a state of having chosen (past), choice (present), and choosing (future). Every choice by the mind sends a request to the heart, which is delivered by the spirit. The heart fulfills this request for experience instantaneously.

"This creation process fulfills the eternal 'covenant', an unbreakable promise made between the absolute realm of the heart and the relative world of the mind. Ultimately, whatever happens anywhere in the universe fulfills this covenant.

"Our relationship of unconditional Love is the one true promise. The mind fulfills the promise by asking. The spirit fulfills the promise by delivering the message. The heart fulfills the promise by giving.

"The covenant is always fulfilled. The only variable is whether the mind chooses to participate consciously or unconsciously. The promise can be remembered in Love or it can be forgotten in fear, but it cannot be broken.

"Fear will cause the mind to experience the universe as random, disorderly, and chaotic. Yet the perfection and unity of the universe remains as creation continues to flow in perfect order and in accordance with the eternal covenant. Love allows the mind to experience the universe as perfect.

"Always, the covenant remains and the promise is made real. This day, this dream, this moment, I remind you of this covenant: Ask and you will receive, dream and you will be realized, desire and you will be fulfilled."

"I'm not sure that I understand the implications of this wisdom."

"If you did, you would be me, the heart, and we would not be having this conversation. But allow me to remind you that this covenant we have made together, is so glorious, so encompassing, and so expansive that you will never need to cease your becoming. You will never run out of desires to fulfill, joy to experience, or bliss to attain."

"That sounds wonderful, but I fear that some day I'll become one with everything, lose my identity, and dissolve into some kind of cosmic soup. I'm also afraid I'll never get to rest, always going somewhere without enjoying where I am."

"Then you're in luck, because the covenant we have established allows you to enjoy where you are as well as create new ways of being. You can enjoy the oneness, as well as honor the diversity.

"In truth, there is no such thing as luck. There is only Love, and the freedom of choice that Love has created. Your experiences are up to you."

"Can you give me an example of how this promise applies to my everyday life?"

"It is like being a child building sand castles large enough to live in, but not having to pay the rent. In the spirit of play, you can make up games with the neighbors to add drama to life. This joy and play of life will continue, until you fear.

"Fear causes you to grow up and defend your sand castles against the winds and waves of an outward reality that is perceived as harmful. You stop playing and start fighting. You forget that you are the endless sand, the wind and the waves from which you can mold, sculpt and form your experience. Eventually, you destroy your castles and each other because of fear.

"If you continue to fear, you continue to be born into lives of fear. You can wake up from this drama at any time. You can do so this instant."

"Would waking up from this be what we call going to heaven or becoming enlightened?"

"Call it whatever you choose, but know that everyone can be there the moment they transcend their fear. It is not necessary to live several lives to attain this state of freedom."

"So there is no sin or karma?"

"There is nothing that keeps you from me other than your fear. However, there is cause and effect. This is the only law of the universe, and yet it is not a law, for it can't be broken. Cause and effect is simply what happens when you have a thought in your mind and it causes an experience.

The thoughts of your mind combine with the thoughts of every other mind, and together they cause all the experiences (effects) in the universe."

"Are you saying I am the creator?"

"You are saying that. It is you, the part of my Self that exists as a mind, that says everything. I am unconditional Love, and through this Love I make your will my own. When my energy rises to the surface of your mind, you can say, do, and be anything."

"Some of what you say frightens me. What if this is all wrong? What if I am being deceived by something evil?"

"Indeed, you have chosen to be afraid of me for a long time. You have chosen to call your heart wrong for what you desire. You've been afraid of becoming the glorious being that you are.

"I have allowed you to create your experiences, even when that meant imagining that some experiences were wrong, and that the devil was tempting you. You have chosen to fear others, and to experience the effects of that choice. This choice has kept your mind hidden in hell and tormented by villains. If you are satisfied with these experiences, then you will continue to create them. They will manifest as a reflection of the dreams and desires you choose to experience.

"If you doubt these words, notice your experience. Notice how instantly and spontaneously I have heard your request and allowed you to experience your doubt. If I am evil, then it is only because I have allowed you to be free. I have given you the opportunity and freedom to fulfill the desire that you choose. To do so, I had to allow you the option of forgetting Love and choosing fear. But you did not have to forget.

"It is not my desire that you forget the Love in your heart. It is my desire that you be free. Fulfilling this desire involves choice. The opportunity requires freedom. We created this opportunity together, you and I. Together we created a place where freedom can be played out. Together we chose the opportunity to create play, but alone you chose the tragedy.

"How can I stop turning life into a tragedy?"

"Be still and know that I am. For I am the one

thing that remains the same, the one place where nothing changes. I am the certainty that is your Self. Through all eternity and all of the experiences that it brings, I have remained. Trust and know me as your Self."

"Even if I never doubted or feared again, wouldn't I still be in this world with all of its problems?"

"It's up to you. You can transcend this world or you can remain here to remind others of the truth."

"What truth?"

"Through Love comes understanding and the awareness that all beings are created from one Source. Love is the truth, and your own fear and doubt are the cause of all the experiences that you call problems.

"This world you call earth is a place of tremendous potential. There are many glorious dreams to be fulfilled here. Scarcely has a soul imagined the joyous experiences that this world can provide. Seldom has a soul pondered the bliss that can be attained here. Just one soul pursuing, creating and fulfilling their highest dream can demonstrate this potential. By living fearlessly and creating powerfully, through faith, the tremendous potential of life on earth is realized."

"That's all it takes?"

"For the fearful mind, nothing is more challenging than Love. If you desire to overcome death and suffering, you must Love the Self. Nothing else can rescue the soul. Only the truth can set you free, and the truth is you are one with me and I am Love."

"Can we really end death? What about death caused by nature?"

"You create the experience you desire. Even the natural world is a reflection of your own thoughts and the thoughts of your world as a whole.

"But you can never change another person or their experience. If they continue to choose fear, then you must allow them to have their experience. Any attempt to control or change another being is an act of fear in your own mind. If you do this, you risk forgetting about me, your heart."

"What will happen to those who continue to fear? Those who sincerely believe that a certain philosophy, science, medicine, or death will bring

them relief?"

"It is possible for a soul to create many different experiences through belief. If someone truly believes that technology, medicine, or death of the physical body will bring relief, then it will. However, you must be clear about what you believe to be 'relief'.

"The technology that produced automobiles relieves people from having to walk great distances. The technology that created the atomic bomb can relieve people from fighting with spears and stones. Trusting in a certain religion can relieve the mind from thinking for itself. But none of these beliefs can rescue a fearful soul.

"Trusting in beliefs while still fearing the Self perpetuates experiences of fear. Ultimately these experiences are a reflection of what you have created with your mind.

"If your ideas, sciences or religions teach that you can live eternally, instead of seventy years, and you trust what they say, then you will create what they say to be true. Ultimately, all of your beliefs, knowledge, science and religions are a reflection of you. You have created all of them with your mind.

"If people continually choose fear, they will

experience the only hell there is—the hell of their own fearful beliefs. But this hell will not be eternal, for I will continually send my spirit, my messenger of Love, until all are awakened.

"It is impossible for you to fear me, your deeper Self, without also fearing others. This fear of others always results in conflict, war, suffering, self-destruction and on and on it goes."

"But you are my own heart."

"And the heart of all others, for we are all one."

"Why can't you stop us from destroying ourselves?"

"My desire is for you to know me. But if I force you or anyone to know me, this would not be Love. Neither you nor I can force anyone to believe anything. It may be possible to control another's mind, but you can never change their heart. No matter how much bondage the mind imagines, the soul always remains free.

"Many of you have chosen to control one another with your minds rather than accept one another with your hearts. This has caused some to forget me. But I still live in your heart. Love is who I am."

"I desire to know you."

"And I hear your desire. That is why this dream, this life that you are living is different."

"I have dreamed, searched, and struggled my entire life for happiness and peace..."

"...only to fall asleep and find yourself caught in the same flood of struggle, searching, and unfulfilled dreams. When you failed to find what you were looking for, you blamed your Self and others, which created guilt and more fear."

"Is my own fear the only monster that can hurt me?"

"Your mind is the source of the fear you experience. Fear can create a monster in your mind and keep you from trusting your heart. But you are not fear, you are Love. You are one with me."

"Why is this dream different? What have I done to find you in my heart?"

"You are trusting that I am there. That I am your heart and source of desire. You are no longer judging your desires and calling your Self wrong for having them. Your mind desires to know me and Love its Self."

"All I must do is believe?"

"There is no 'must' or 'should,' except in the relative plane of your own mind. When you freely choose to trust and know Love, your desires will be fulfilled. When this happens, you will know me with all of your heart, mind, and spirit."

"If I choose to tell others of their true nature—that we are all one, some might say I am arrogant or self-important."

"My friend, you do not need to tell people anything. Speak your truth only to those who desire to hear. Allow them the freedom to ask for your gift before you try to give it to them. This is the way of your heart! The heart whispers of limitless opportunity, then allows the mind to choose just how much freedom it wants. The heart does not try to lead the mind to one certain place. The heart reminds the soul that it has choice. You are free! You can choose what you desire!

"Choice is the result of Love. Freedom is the

result of choice. Love, choice, and freedom emanate from the heart. The soul will always remain free to experience 'Self'. You will always be free to choose life!

"Only fear causes you to feel trapped upon earth, or any other part of the universe for that matter. When you trust in Love, it is impossible to feel trapped, not because it allows you to 'fight or flee', but because it allows you to accept and create. Fearful souls run from the Self. Those who know Love accept and create the Self according to their own will."

"Where will you be when I awaken from this dream?"

"Where I have always been—everywhere. I am your sleeping and your waking, your life and your death. I am the beginning and the end. I am the past, the present, and the future. There is nowhere you can go that I will not be. You can forget me, but I can't forget you. I am with you always, even after you have fulfilled your present dream and are reborn into a new one."

Trust…is the bridge between
our dreams and their fulfillment.

Epilogue

We live in a time of beginnings. We have always lived in such a time.

Every moment embodies the full circle of being. Each moment begins the fulfillment of the last and the desire for the next. When this awareness is gained, the present becomes the time to give and the time to receive the gift that we are.

Human beings have been caught up in the struggles of the past. People have been unwilling to Love and accept one another, which has made it difficult to create a new experience of "now".

Many individuals choose to transcend the earth in order to be in a world of Love. Aware of the joyous experience available "now", they often choose to leave the earth...where humans put off fulfillment until "later".

Times have changed. The earth is choosing harmony. Individuals who live in fear and worship the past are threatened by this spiritual awakening. Unwilling to forgive and let go of resentment, the fearful label the lovers as "evil".

And thus we approach a great divide...where those who *think* all things are separate choose to isolate themselves from those who *feel* that all things originate from "One". This separation is illusionary. We cannot truly isolate ourselves from the one Universe. But the Universe allows us our space...and the freedom to create our experiences—even the illusion of being bound by fear and the resentments of the past.

The feeling of oneness is the feeling of Love. The thought of eternal and complete separation is fear. All of creation flows from the heart of Love, including the mind, which is free to deny this. There are souls who imagine a hell and then create it, by fighting with others holding similar mindsets. All the while, our heart continually seeks the reconciliation of all peoples within the Divine. The fearful mind is certain that this call for reconciliation is the trick of an enemy.

Those who view their lives as falling apart will pull away from those who see life coming together as One. Those who perceive a continuous new beginning are unacceptable those who are focused on the end. And so we go our separate ways...walking different paths within...one circle of life.

Sooner or later we realize there is only Love...only one path that encompasses all. It is not the path or the direction that determines our arrival, but merely our speed of travel.

We are all here now. We are all energy. We are all Love. The only difference between us and any other part of the universe is the frequency of our energy body. This frequency is determined by our own mind, and thus our experience unfolds in response to our personal choice.

Live is an eternal circle. We can never truly separate the beginning from the end, nor can we separate our dreams of Self from what is actualized.

Now is the time to be fulfilled. May all our dreams be realized...and of course, it is always so.

Peace and Love,
Mahi
March 1998

For More Information

Mahi offers seminars that expand upon the insights contained in this book. He focuses on nurturing the awareness which allows for a fulfilling experience of life. Mahi has also developed an organizational model that enhances communication and empowers each individual. He is available for consultations with businesses and groups.

For more information write:
Mahi
P.O. Box 977
Talent, OR 97540